Arctic Animals

Puffins

ABDO
Publishing Company

Big
Buddy BOOKS
Arctic Animals

by Julie Murray

VISIT US AT
www.abdopublishing.com

Published by ABDO Publishing Company, PO Box 398166, Minneapolis, Minnesota 55439.

Printed in the United States of America, North Mankato, Minnesota.
032013
012014

♻ PRINTED ON RECYCLED PAPER

Coordinating Series Editor: Rochelle Baltzer
Editor: Marcia Zappa
Contributing Editors: Megan M. Gunderson, Sarah Tieck
Graphic Design: Maria Hosley
Cover Photograph: *iStockphoto*: ©iStockphoto.com/PaulTessier.
Interior Photographs/Illustrations: *Getty Images*: Steven Kazlowski (pp. 7, 13), Michael Sewell (p. 7); *Glow Images*: Wayne Barrett & Anne MacKay (p. 17), Glen Bartley (p. 8), Richard Costin/FLPA (p. 27), Jared Hobbs (p. 12), John Warden (p. 13); *iStockphoto*: ©iStockphoto.com/JoeGough (p. 25), ©iStockphoto.com/nailzchap (p. 9), ©iStockphoto.com/powerofforever (p. 15), ©iStockphoto.com/tirc83 (p. 25); *Minden Pictures*: Mike Jones/FLPA (p. 23); *Photo Researchers, Inc.*: Bryan and Cherry Alexander (pp. 15, 19), Mark Boulton (p. 23); *Shutterstock*: Galyna Andrushko (p. 9), Mircea BEZERGHEANU (pp. 5, 13), John M. Fugett (p. 11), gabrisigno (p. 21), Matthew Jacques (p. 4), Mary Lane (p. 29), Maksimilian (p. 10), mlorenz (p. 11), Christopher Wood (p. 4).

Library of Congress Cataloging-in-Publication Data

Murray, Julie, 1969-
 Puffins / Julie Murray.
   p. cm. -- (Arctic animals)
 Audience: 007-011.
  ISBN 978-1-61783-800-2
1. Puffins--Juvenile literature. I. Title.
 QL696.C42M87 2014
 598.3'3--dc23
                            2012049645

Contents

Earth has many different **regions**. But, few stand out as much as the Arctic. This is the northernmost part of Earth. The area is known for its freezing cold weather and great sheets of ice.

Puffins are known for their large, bright bills. They are also called "sea parrots."

The Arctic includes land from several **continents**. It also includes the Arctic Ocean and the huge sea of ice that floats on it. The Arctic is home to many interesting animals. One of these is the puffin.

Puffin Territory

There are three kinds of puffins. Atlantic puffins live in the southern Arctic Ocean and the northern Atlantic Ocean. Horned and tufted puffins live in the southern Arctic Ocean and the northern Pacific Ocean.

Puffins spend much of their lives on open ocean waters. During the **mating** season in the spring and summer, they head for land. They lay their eggs on islands and coasts.

Atlantic Puffin Territory

Horned Puffin Territory

Tufted Puffin Territory

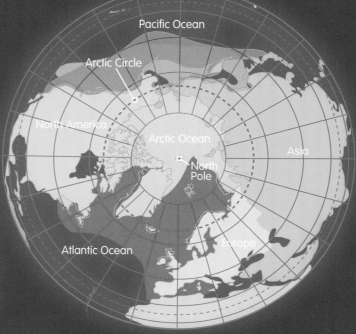

Pacific Ocean

Arctic Circle

North America

Arctic Ocean

North Pole

Asia

Atlantic Ocean

Europe

Many Atlantic puffins live far into the Arctic region. They face cold, snow, and ice much of the year.

Horned and tufted puffins (*right*) are sometimes found as far south as California and Japan.

Welcome to the Arctic!

If you took a trip to where puffins live, you might find…

…seabirds.

Puffins aren't the only birds that live in freezing Arctic waters. There are more than 60 different types. These include gulls, loons, ducks, alcids, and skuas (*left*). Puffins are part of the alcid family.

Gulf of Alaska

BEAUFORT SEA

Ar

GREENLAND

(Kalaallit Nunaat)

GREENLAND SEA

Dav

LABRADOR SEA

nmark Strait

NORWEGIAN SEA

SEA OF OKHOTSK

LAPTEV SEA

'C OCEAN

North Pole

BARENTS SEA

Cape

A

S

...the Arctic Ocean.

Many puffins live in the Arctic Ocean. This ocean covers the northern part of Earth. It is the smallest ocean on the planet. The northernmost part is covered in ice year-round. Even during the summer, this ice can be up to 15 feet (5 m) thick.

...people.

Puffins avoid people. But, they often nest on land that is part of countries with lots of people. These include the United States, Canada, the United Kingdom, Russia, and Japan. Puffins are popular with people in the areas where they live.

Take a Closer Look

Puffins have small, rounded bodies covered in feathers. They have short legs with **webbed** feet. They keep their large wings tucked into their bodies while resting. A puffin has small, dark eyes. It has a large, triangle-shaped bill.

Puffins are small birds. Adults are 7 to 15 inches (18 to 38 cm) tall. Their wings are 20 to 25 inches (51 to 64 cm) from tip to tip. A puffin weighs 12 to 32 ounces (340 to 907 g).

Tufted puffins (*right*) are the largest types of puffins. Atlantic puffins are the smallest.

Countershading helps keep Atlantic and horned puffins safe from predators. From above, their black backs blend in with the dark water. From below, their white bellies blend in with the bright sky.

Atlantic (*right*) and horned (*above*) puffins have white feathers on their bellies, chests, and faces. They have black feathers on their backs, wings, and tails.

11

Looking Good

Puffins are known for their colorful, interesting appearances. But, they don't look that way all the time. During the spring, puffins change to get ready for **mating**. Their legs get brighter. Their bills grow colorful plates. And, each type of puffin grows special decorations. Scientists think this helps puffins find mates.

After mating, puffins begin to lose their decorations. Their legs and bills become dull. And, their faces get darker.

Puffins look very different during the mating and non-mating seasons. Scientists once thought they were different types of birds!

Tufted puffins grow two gold strips of feathers during mating season. These run from above the eyes to the back of the neck.

Atlantic puffin bills become blue, yellow, and reddish-orange during mating season. These birds also get bright yellow or orange spots on the sides of their mouths.

Horned puffins get a pointed black growth above each eye during mating season. These growths are called horns because of their shape.

13

Water, Land, and Air

   Puffins spend their lives on water and land. They can swim, walk, and fly.

   Puffins are especially good at swimming and diving. They use their powerful wings to paddle underwater. They use their **webbed** feet to change direction.

When resting, puffins float high on the water.

Puffins are well built for their watery lives. They can drink salt water. And, their waterproof feathers keep their bodies dry.

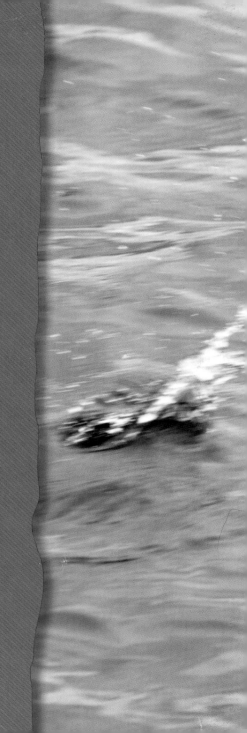

Puffins are not as good at walking or flying. A puffin's short legs are located toward the back of its body. So, it is somewhat unsteady walking on land.

Puffins fly fast. They can reach speeds up to 55 miles (89 km) per hour. But, they must beat their wings very quickly to stay in the air. Sometimes, they beat them as many as 400 times a minute! And, puffins often crash when landing.

Puffins take off for flight by diving off a cliff or running. Sometimes, they run across the surface of water before flying.

Mealtime

Puffins are **carnivores**. They mostly eat small fish, such as herring, sand eels, and capelins. Adult puffins also eat crabs, squid, sea urchins, and worms.

Puffins dive from the air or the surface of the water to catch their food. They can dive hundreds of feet. Adult puffins eat their food underwater.

Puffins usually stay underwater for about 20 to 30 seconds.

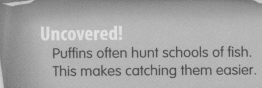

Uncovered!
Puffins often hunt schools of fish.
This makes catching them easier.

Social Life

During **mating** season, puffins are **social** animals. They live in groups called colonies. Colonies can be very small or very large.

Puffins mostly use actions to **communicate**. Puffin mates often rub their bills together. If a puffin is unhappy, it puffs up its feathers. Then, it opens its wings and bill. When puffins fight, they lock bills and try to knock each other over.

Uncovered!

Adult puffins make low, purring noises while flying. They make loud growling noises on land. And, young puffins peep.

Puffins often gather in colonies on islands and cliffs near coasts.

Incredible Eggs

Before laying eggs, puffin **mates** dig a **burrow** near the ocean. They choose a spot that is hard for predators to reach. This is usually the side of a grassy hill or a rocky cliff.

Inside the burrow, the pair builds a nest of feathers and grass. The female lays one egg in the nest. The mates take turns keeping the egg warm. They tuck it under one wing and lean against it. After about six weeks, the egg **hatches**.

Uncovered!
Puffins usually keep the same mate their whole lives.

Puffin eggs can be white, off-white, or light gray. They sometimes have brown, light purple, or light blue spots.

Puffins often use old burrows from earlier years.

Baby Puffins

Baby puffins are called chicks. Puffin chicks stay in their **burrows**. Their parents feed them by catching small fish and bringing them to the burrow.

After about 40 days, puffin parents leave their chicks to **survive** on their own. At this time, the parents head back to the open ocean.

Uncovered!

Puffin parents carry fish to their chicks in their bills. They usually carry around 10 fish at a time. But, scientists have seen them carry more than 60!

Young puffins (*left*) look similar to adult puffins during the non-mating season. They don't have bright colors or decorations.

A puffin parent uses its tongue to hold fish against the top of its bill. Then, it can open its bill to catch more fish for its chick.

About a week after their parents leave, puffin chicks are also ready to leave their **burrows**. They leave at night.

Puffin chicks can swim right away, but they can't fly for several more days. Soon, puffin chicks head to the open ocean. They spend two to three years there. Then, they return to the area they were born in to **mate**.

Uncovered!

Scientists aren't sure how puffins find their birthplaces. The birds may use sounds, smells, or sights from the ocean. Or, they may use the stars.

When puffin chicks leave their burrows, they don't have fully grown feathers for flying. So, they walk to or fall into the ocean.

Survivors

Life in the Arctic isn't easy for puffins. Long ago, people commonly hunted them. Today, their predators include rats, foxes, great black-backed gulls, and snowy owls. **Pollution**, fishing, and oil businesses reduce their food supply and harm their **habitats**.

Still, puffins **survive**. People work to make sure they have large, clean places to live. In most areas, their population remains steady. Puffins help make the Arctic an amazing place.

Uncovered!

Herring gulls are also a threat to puffins. They don't hunt adult puffins. But, they steal their prey. And, they steal puffin eggs and chicks from their burrows.

Scientists believe wild puffins live more than 20 years.

Wow!

I'll bet you never knew...

...that the Atlantic puffin's scientific name, *Fratercula arctica*, means "little brother of the north" in Latin.

...that long ago, people believed puffins were a cross between a bird and a fish. They thought this because puffins swim so well underwater.

...that scientists still have a lot to learn about puffins. Scientists use special leg bands to track birds. But, puffins often ruin these bands while digging and swimming. So, scientists aren't able to gather much information about them.

Important Words

burrow an animal's underground home.

carnivore (KAHR-nuh-vawr) an animal or a plant that eats meat.

communicate (kuh-MYOO-nuh-kayt) to share knowledge, thoughts, or feelings.

continent one of Earth's seven main land areas.

habitat a place where a living thing is naturally found.

hatch to be born from an egg.

mate to join as a couple in order to reproduce, or have babies. A mate is a partner to join with in order to reproduce.

pollution human waste that dirties or harms air, water, or land.

region a large part of the world that is different from other parts.

social (SOH-shuhl) naturally living or growing in groups.

survive to continue to live or exist.

webbed having toes that are joined together with skin, or webs.

Web Sites

To learn more about puffins, visit ABDO Publishing Company online. Web sites about puffins are featured on our Book Links page. These links are routinely monitored and updated to provide the most current information available.

www.abdopublishing.com

Index